In loving memory

_____

_____

_____

_____

_____

_____

_____

_____

_____

_____

_____

In loving memory

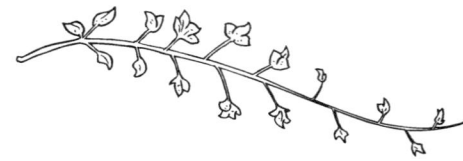

_____

_____

_____

_____

_____

_____

_____

_____

_____

_____

_____

In loving memory

In loving memory

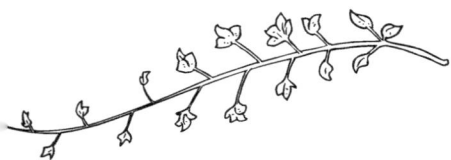

In loving memory

_____

_____

_____

_____

_____

_____

_____

_____

_____

_____

_____

In loving memory

In loving memory

In loving memory

In loving memory

In loving memory

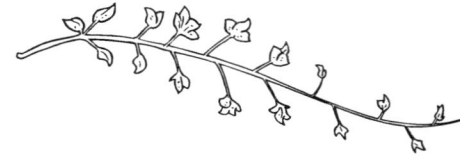

In loving memory

In loving memory

In loving memory

_____

_____

_____

_____

_____

_____

_____

_____

_____

_____

_____

In loving memory

In loving memory

In loving memory

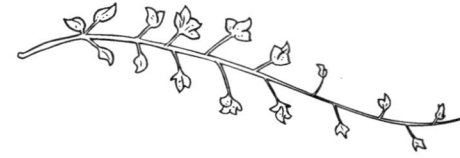

In loving memory

In loving memory

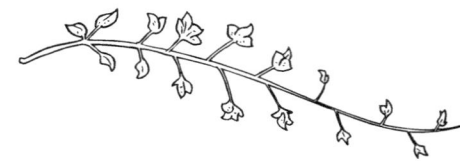

In loving memory

In loving memory

In loving memory

In loving memory

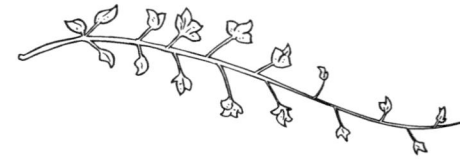

_____

_____

_____

_____

_____

_____

_____

_____

_____

_____

_____

_____

In loving memory

In loving memory

In loving memory

In loving memory

In loving memory

In loving memory

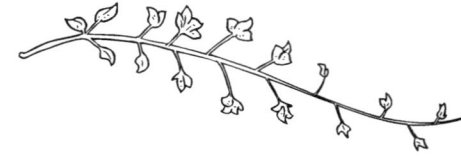

In loving memory

_____

_____

_____

_____

_____

_____

_____

_____

_____

_____

_____

_____

In loving memory

In loving memory

_____

_____

_____

_____

_____

_____

_____

_____

_____

_____

_____

In loving memory

_____

_____

_____

_____

_____

_____

_____

_____

_____

_____

_____

_____

In loving memory

_____

_____

_____

_____

_____

_____

_____

_____

_____

_____

_____

_____

In loving memory

In loving memory

_____

_____

_____

_____

_____

_____

_____

_____

_____

_____

_____

_____

In loving memory

In loving memory

In loving memory

In loving memory

In loving memory

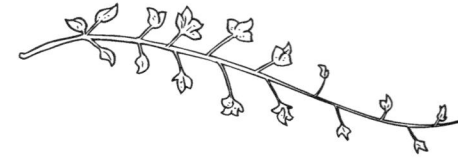

In loving memory

_____

_____

_____

_____

_____

_____

_____

_____

_____

_____

_____

In loving memory

In loving memory

In loving memory

In loving memory

_____

_____

_____

_____

_____

_____

_____

_____

_____

_____

_____

In loving memory

In loving memory

In loving memory

_____

_____

_____

_____

_____

_____

_____

_____

_____

_____

_____

In loving memory

_____

_____

_____

_____

_____

_____

_____

_____

_____

_____

_____

In loving memory

_____

_____

_____

_____

_____

_____

_____

_____

_____

_____

_____

www.ingramcontent.com/pod-product-compliance
Lightning Source LLC
Chambersburg PA
CBHW041653260326

41914CB00018B/1629